YOU AND THE BIBLE

(Formerly *The Bible Today*)

Tough Questions and Straight Answers

Patrick Kaler, C.SS.R.

One Liguori Drive
Liguori, Missouri 63057
(314) 464-2500

Imprimi Potest:
John F. Dowd, C.SS.R.
Provincial, St. Louis Province
Redemptorist Fathers

Imprimatur:
+ Edward J. O'Donnell
Vicar General, Archdiocese of St. Louis

ISBN 0-89243-240-3

Copyright © 1985, Liguori Publications
All rights reserved.
Printed in U.S.A.

Scripture texts used in this work are taken from the NEW AMERICAN BIBLE, copyright © 1970, by the Confraternity of Christian Doctrine, Washington, D.C., and are used by permission of copyright owner. All rights reserved.

Excerpts from THE DOCUMENTS OF VATICAN II, Abbott-Gallagher edition, reprinted with permission of America Press, Inc., 106 West 56 Street, New York, NY 10019, ©1966. All rights reserved.

Excerpts from the English translation of THE ROMAN MISSAL ©1983, International Committee on English in the Liturgy, Inc. All rights reserved.

Excerpts from THE CHURCH AND THE SYNAGOGUE, reprinted with permission from National Catholic News Service, 1312 Massachusetts Avenue, N.W., Washington, DC 20005.

The questions and answers contained herein were originally published as "Dear Padre" bulletins. Our thanks to the editors of the Liguori Sunday Bulletins for their kind permission to reprint these topics as they appear here.

Table of Contents

1. How the Bible Got to Us 5
2. Where on Earth the Bible Came from 7
3. The Role of Poets and Historians 12
4. How the Bible Speaks to Us 15
5. The Presence of Errors 17
6. A Different Kind of History 19
7. A Record of Growth 22
8. Those "Missing Books" 24
9. The "Old Laws" 26
10. The "Boring" Parts 29
11. "Yahweh" and "Jehovah" 32
12. Scandalous Violence 35
13. The Word on Abortion 37
14. The Gospels and the Risen Christ 40
15. The Good News in Four Versions 46
16. Those "Lives of Christ" 49
17. Blaming the Jews 51
18. Jesus' Brothers and Sisters 54
19. The Protestant Lord's Prayer 56
20. The End Time 59
21. Paraclete: What Does It Mean? 61

1. How the Bible Got to Us

> On a recent trip to Washington, D.C., I was impressed by the protection provided for the original Declaration of Independence . . . the tinted glass that filtered the light and the special mechanism that lowered it into a huge safe at nighttime. What about the original Scriptures? They are much older — what condition are they in? Where are they kept? Are they in a section of the Vatican Library or in a special building in Jerusalem? Can an ordinary person go see them or is special permission required?

It might shock you: We don't have any of the original manuscripts of Sacred Scripture. They are all lost. All we have are copies. In fact, it would be more accurate to say that all we have are copies of copies.

> How could the religious leaders of the past allow this to happen? How could they allow these precious documents (the originals or even the copies) to be lost or destroyed? One would think that they would have laid down their lives protecting them.

The truth is, they may well have died trying to save them. A little background will help us see what probably happened.

First, with regard to the material of the manuscripts themselves — the original text and the earliest copies were written on papyrus. This was a thin, paperlike product made from a kind of marsh reed that grew principally in the Nile Delta. This fragile material stood little chance of survival in any but the driest of climates. Humidity and time were major enemies of such manuscripts — and that included all the biblical originals and all copies made before the fourth century B.C., when more durable parchment (treated animal hides) replaced papyrus. Parchment was used until about the tenth century, when paper became the common writing material.

But history informs us that the priceless biblical texts had even more dangerous enemies — violence-prone human beings. Because of its strategic location in the Middle East, the Holy Land frequently became the battleground where competing armies clashed. The whole country was laid waste repeatedly. Numerous ancient copies of the Old Testament, or parts thereof, must have been lost during the destructions of Jerusalem and its temple by the Babylonians in 587 B.C. and by the Romans in A.D. 70.

But not only did the general destruction of war take its toll of the sacred scrolls, they became pinpointed targets as well! Around 175 B.C., Antiochus IV, one of the heirs to Alexander the Great's divided empire, became so intent on imposing Greek culture on the Jewish people that he made the Jewish Scriptures the object of search-and-destroy missions. And his example led to similar destructiveness in many synagogues scattered throughout the Greco-Roman world.

Until 1947, our oldest complete copies of the Hebrew Bible were those made in the ninth and tenth centuries A.D. But what happened between 1947 and 1956 changed all that. During those years over six hundred scrolls and thousands of scroll fragments were discovered in eleven caves in the very arid Dead Sea area. About one third of these were biblical writings. Although only the scroll of Isaiah was found complete, the fragments provided snatches and bits of almost all the other Old Testament books. The best news of all: Some of these manuscripts date as early as 150 B.C. That makes them the most ancient surviving texts.

While there are no complete New Testament texts from earlier than the fourth century A.D., we do have some fragments dating from the second century. The most sensational one is the postage-stamp-size John Rylands Papyrus, discovered in Egypt in 1920. It proved to contain a text identifiable as John 18:31-33 on one side and John 18:37-38 on the other side. Because it's dated about A.D. 130, it's the oldest bit of New Testament writing in our possession.

But since we do not have the original inspired writings, only copies of copies, can we trust the Bible we are holding in our hands? How faithful is our text to the original wording?

Thanks to the patient and devoted labor of historians and linguists, believers as well as nonbelievers, we have nothing to worry about. One New Testament expert put it this way: "Ninety percent of the New Testament text is certainly established. In the remaining ten percent, variations of any consequence are few and far between." The same could be said for the Old Testament. That means that we can affirm, along with all the world's scholars, that our Bible is, practically speaking, identical with the inspired original. For that we are forever grateful.

2. Where on Earth the Bible Came from

Every now and then I hear of archaeologists making important discoveries in the Holy Land. What effect are these finds having on what we think of the stories in the Bible?

In recent years biblical archaeology has come into its own. One reason is that the current Israeli government is itself very interested in what might lie buried beneath its topsoil. Besides developing its own expert teams, the State of Israel has warmly welcomed many foreign professionals and qualified amateurs who have appeared on its shores with pick and shovel in hand. The payoff — in archaeological treasures — has been the richest the world has ever seen. It's an exciting time to be a biblical researcher.

But this does not mean that all this digging is seeking or finding anything that will have any impact on anyone's acceptance of the biblical text and message. If you start with the faith acknowledgment that the Bible is *the Word of God,* you can expect to understand that Word better by studying the world in which the Bible stories take place. If you start without faith, digging alone won't supply it.

Because the Bible tells the stories of human beings who lived in a world very different from our own, recent discoveries take on considerable significance. Every time a scholar dates a bit of pottery, unravels the secrets of a tattered parchment, or deciphers the scratchings on an ancient tablet, a few more pieces fall into place in our picture of the biblical past. Solid artifacts that can be handled, measured, and weighed also add a touch of realism that is sometimes lacking in our attitude toward the sacred text. That, certainly, is no small blessing.

Will archaeology help us to better understand the story of Christ's life?

Most of the significant finds of recent years relate to Old Testament times. The Hebrew Scriptures are the chronicle of a people with a very lengthy history. Such a nation would naturally have left many material traces that could be unearthed. But it's a different story with regard to the beginnings of Christianity. The time span is not millenia but several decades. The followers of Jesus would have left few artifacts that can be dug up. That's why most New Testament archaeology illustrates only the social, political, and cultural environment in which Jesus and his followers lived. But, even so, this filling in of the background can be quite informative. Let's take a brief look at a few of these discoveries.

Visitors to the Holy Land are invariably taken to see the impressive synagogue ruins at Capernaum on the northern shore of the Lake of Galilee. This is not the synagogue in which Jesus preached and healed (John 6:59; Mark 1:21) but one that dates from the fifth century A.D. However, since such synagogues were usually built on the foundation of earlier structures this probably is the correct site for the gospel scenes. Eighty-four feet south of this is an octagonal fifth-century church; under it excavators found signs of several centuries of buildings that could be called housechurches, going back to what was a first-century house. This residence, the excavators have good reason for maintaining, was the house of Peter mentioned in Mark 1:29. Better than that, they think they have found the very room that Jesus himself used whenever he stayed with his chief apostle.

How can they say that it was Jesus' room?

Perhaps as early as the middle of first-century A.D. the dark basalt floor, walls, and ceiling of this room were plastered over. In ancient Capernaum this would have been most unusual. Also, before this period the pottery found there was like that found in rooms designated for domestic use — cooking pots and bowls. Once the room was plastered only storage jars and broken lamps are found. Everything suggests that this room, previously part of a private home, was now devoted to some kind of public use. That would have happened only if this, indeed, had been Jesus' room. It is also the earliest evidence for Christian gatherings that has yet come to light.

Can we now definitely locate Calvary and the tomb from which Jesus arose?

We've always known that a place of execution and a burial site had to be outside the city — the Gospels indicate this and the Jewish custom of the time demanded this. But scholars have had difficulties with the exact position of Jerusalem's walls at the time of Christ.

The Jewish historian Josephus speaks of three defensive walls encircling Jerusalem. The first wall was built either by David or

Solomon, and the third was begun by Herod Agrippa I in the A.D. 40s. The second wall would have been standing during Jesus' ministry; it included more of the city than the first but much less than the third. In the early fourth century, Emperor Constantine built the Church of the Resurrection on a site that was, he believed, outside this second wall. The site had long been venerated by Christians as the place of Christ's death and burial. Later on, the Basilica of the Holy Sepulcher was built on the same spot; it enclosed both Calvary and the tomb under one roof. But for some time, some scholars believed that the site of the basilica placed it within the approximate line of the second old wall, and they therefore rejected the traditional Holy Sepulcher's claims. They even proposed an alternate site. However, recent discoveries place the traditional site well outside the most probable course of the second wall and thus support its authenticity. Moreover, there are indications that much of the stone for the wall (and for other constructions) was quarried right there, that is, that this site was originally a major quarry for the city.

Scholar David O'Rourke, in his book *The Holy Land as Jesus Knew It* (Liguori Publications), suggests the following scenario: "As they [the quarrymen] cut into the stone, layer by layer, they discovered that part of it was flawed. There was a cracked and inferior section . . . unusable for building blocks. So the workers . . . cut around it . . . it would be a pointless waste of a good quarry site to abandon the whole place because of the flaw. When they had finished with their quarrying they had partly cleared out a new space outside the walls . . . within it stood that section of flawed stone, an outcropping rising about thirty feet from the floor of the quarry to where the top of the hill had been. At the perimeter were the flat, stone surfaces of the quarry walls. It was not long before these man-made bluffs were put to a use quite common in the Jerusalem area. Holes were cut into the walls, chambers large enough to entomb the bodies of the dead. . . .

"Shortly after the days of King Herod this quarry was put to another, more grisly use . . . The flawed stone . . . formed a little hill, high enough to be seen by passersby. Here criminals were put to death. An upright beam was fixed in the flawed stone. The poor unfortunates sentenced to crucifixion . . . would be brought here dragging a shorter beam along with them. Their arms would be tied to the short beam, it would be hoisted to the top of the fixed upright, and they would be left there.''

What else have we learned about the crucifixion?

Despite the many references to crucifixion in the New Testament and in Jewish and secular literature, until recently we didn't have any firsthand *archaeological* evidence of that gruesome punishment. But in 1968 some Israeli experts came across an ossuary (bone box) in a first-century tomb near Jerusalem. The inscription on the lid identified the contents as the bones of a Jewish man named Yehohanan and his small son. Once the box was opened it was obvious that the adult had been crucified. Although we can't reconstruct the poor man's precise position as he hung upon the cross, it's clear that the two nails used for the hands were actually driven through the wrists. We also know that only one nail had been used to fasten his legs, because the single large iron spike was still imbedded in the two heel bones. Moreover, the shin bones had been *intentionally* broken. This illustrates a scene similar to John 19:32. The Fourth Gospel points out the similarity of Jesus to the Passover lamb in his not having his bones broken. But Yehohanan's deliberately fractured bones give concrete nonliterary evidence that such a practice did at times accompany crucifixion in first-century Palestine.

I hope that these details serve to give you some sense of reality that archaeology can provide for our encounter with the Word of God. It makes us realize how much the key events interpreted in the Bible are facts of human history. We sometimes, in effect, pigeonhole these happenings as things somehow separated from reality, as our parish church is from our home and Sunday is from the rest of the week.

3. The Role of Poets and Historians

I've just started a Bible study course and already I've come across a term that I don't fully understand — "literary forms." Could you explain it to me in nice, simple English?

I'll be happy to try. It should be easy because, even though you might not realize it, you deal with "literary forms" or "genres" every day and, I presume, handle them quite well. It has always been that way. In fact, you've done so for a long time. Remember when you were small? When you were busy learning your letters and numbers, if someone would say "Once upon a time . . ." what happened? Immediately and without even thinking about it your whole attitude changed, and your face took on the look of expectation reserved for fairy tales. Special doors in your mind swung open so all the wondrous truth and beauty of the fairy-tale world could flood your heart. Already at that early age you had learned that the first step to understanding all human communication was the proper identification of the form, or genre, being used.

But what about stories that deal with real life situations?

You mean like those appearing in the newspaper? What are you looking for when you glance at the front page? You are looking for the "straight news" — the details and facts of today's events without party-line praise or criticism. When you turn to the editorial page, you expect something else — not only the raw facts but certain people's opinions and interpretations of those facts. You shift again when you come upon the adventures of Charlie

Brown, Garfield, or Hagar in the comic section. You adapt to other literary forms when you glance over the advertisements, Dear Abby, the want ads, or the obituary notices. This type of mental shifting goes on all day long. Turn on the TV, the same process continues — you watch the Muppets differently from the evening news, a situation comedy differently from a serious documentary.

What does this have to do with Sacred Scripture?

The answer is: everything! Why? Because the Bible is the Word of God *in human language*. That means it takes on all the characteristics of human speech and communication. And we know that no human word can exist by itself within a vacuum; it must always be part of a given "literary form." So, as we open the Bible we see spread before us a complete smorgasbord of the different literary forms. Within its covers can be found the whole spectrum of types familiar to us, plus a few that are specific to the ancient Middle Eastern cultures that made up the biblical world. Within the Scriptures we can come across lengthy historical accounts, full-blown national epics, colorful stories and challenging parables, lyrical poems and rich liturgical hymns, detailed law codes, personal and group letters, a treasury of wisdom writings, proverbs and prophecies, and, not the least, powerful prayers suitable for almost every occasion. This list does not claim to be exhaustive; there are divisions within each division.

How does this affect my reading of the Word of God and my discovery of the truth I expect to find there?

Since each of these modes of expression, each literary form, has its own special kind of truth, the full impact of that truth won't be experienced unless you can correctly identify the particular form in which the truth is contained. And when that happens, lo and behold, you will be primed to experience a special graced event — the comprehending of the specific message God wished to communicate through these very limited, human words. On the other hand, when the reader is mistaken about the literary form of a biblical passage his or her reception of the truth is affected — it doesn't come through to him or her as God intended it to. Such a mistake will almost certainly lead to a serious misinterpretation. Frequently, the result is that God's Word is twisted and misapplied — some people using it even to justify hurtful actions against their neighbors.

Is this just your view or is it the generally accepted Catholic view?

I'm glad you asked. Vatican II urges: "Those who search out the intention of the sacred writers must, among other things, have regard for 'literary forms.' For truth is proposed and expressed in a variety of ways, depending on whether a text is history of one kind or another, or whether its form is that of prophecy, poetry, or some other type of speech. The interpreter must investigate what meaning the sacred writer intended to express and actually expressed in particular circumstances as he used contemporary literary forms in accordance with the situation of his own time and culture. For the correct understanding of what the sacred author wanted to assert, due attention must be paid to the customary and characteristic styles of perceiving, speaking, and narrating which prevailed at the time of the sacred writer, and to the customs men normally followed at that period in their everyday dealings with one another" (Dogmatic Constitution on Divine Revelation, #12).

This is the way to go about getting out of Scripture what Paul wished for a group of early Christians: "I commend you now to the Lord, and to that gracious word of his which can enlarge you, and give you a share among all who are consecrated to him" (Acts 20:32).

4. How the Bible Speaks to Us

I've been reading the Bible for spiritual nourishment. But I'm not sure if I should continue. A friend of mine got involved with the Bible and has now left the Church. I don't want that to happen to me. But does this mean that I have to give up my daily Bible reading?

I'll bet that many Catholics hunger for the Bible, and yet are concerned that they might fall into error in interpreting it. Scholar George Montague addresses this question: "Can Christians who have not done lengthy studies legitimately interpret Scripture as a personal word from the Lord? We know that private interpretation can lead to both theoretical and practical error. Besides, Catholics have learned from childhood that the teaching authority of the Church is the only authentic interpreter of Scripture. . . . Even so, is there some way we can affirm our experience of the power of God's word without abandoning the necessary protection of objective controls in Scripture interpretation?"

Father Montague thinks that the key is the biblical idea of prophecy. He remarks that while the popular understanding of prophecy has to do with speaking, its more basic meaning is a matter of *hearing* God's Word (Isaiah 50:4). Sometimes this involves hearing a word that is to be addressed to others, but often is addressed to the prophet himself for his own understanding of what the Lord is doing in his life. "As we have seen, this mission to others is not the root of the prophetic experience. The root is hearing God speak, whether for oneself or for others, and this ability to hear God's Word in power is basically what the gift of the Holy Spirit is all about."

But the Scriptures are clear that all prophecy is subject to discernment. We know what can

happen when this is ignored. To use an extreme example, at times good-willed but misguided people have read Mark 16:18 as an invitation to prove their faith by playing with rattlesnakes or drinking cyanide. Against this kind of tragic misreading of God's Word what protection do we have? Are there norms by which we can discern whether our understanding of a text is from the Holy Spirit or from a less trustworthy spirit?

Yes, there are norms. First, we have to discover the literal, historical meaning of the text, the sense the author intended. This involves knowing something about the culture of the time and the literary forms used.

Second, in keeping with Paul's discussion of prophecy (Romans 12:6), any use of a scriptural text should be in harmony with the total message of Scripture and with the apostolic faith handed on in the Church. In a number of places Paul discerns and regulates prophecy (1 Corinthians 14; 2 Thessalonians 2:2) and the evangelists warn against false prophecy (especially Matthew 7:15-23, 24:11).

That's why we should recognize the importance of serious Bible study, of a growing knowledge of our faith, and of submission to proper Church authority, which, incidentally, is as much a gift of the Spirit as any interior and personal inspiration. In a word, our greatest protection is filial allegiance to the Church itself. As Father Montague puts it: "Though a prophetic reading may be only for our own personal nourishment and not for public proclamation, if it is authentically from the Spirit it can only lead to building up the body of the Church in unity and love."

By all means don't stop your prayerful reading of the Bible. I'm sure the Word of God will continue to speak to your heart:

> . . . Lo! I will pour out to you my spirit,
> I will acquaint you with my words (Proverbs 1:23).

5. The Presence of Errors

I have a simple, direct question for you, and I want a straight answer: Are there errors in the Bible? I'd like a simple yes or no answer without anything added to it.

Your question and the conditions you put on my answer remind me of that old trick question: Answer yes or no — Have you stopped beating your wife? The question itself is unfair. It incriminates the husband no matter how he answers, and it completely ignores the truth of the situation. The fact is, some topics are so complex and multilayered that questions about them really cannot be answered in a simple way. In that case, then, a positive or negative monosyllable, standing by itself, is misleading. It doesn't serve the truth, it perpetuates error. In a similar manner, fairness and respect for God's Word require that my answer to your question be more than simply yes or no.

All right then, qualify your answer as you wish. I'll let you know if I think you're avoiding the problem.

It depends on how you view the Bible. One recognized Scripture scholar, Father Martucci, puts it this way: "Everything that the Bible teaches must be taken as a divine teaching and, consequently, as inerrant. But everything is not *taught* in the Bible. Many things are utilized or uttered in the Bible without their being the object of a teaching on the part of the human author and, consequently, on the part of God in whose name he speaks. In other words, everything that the Bible teaches is true, but the biblical authors do not always teach. And even when they teach they do so within limits and from quite definite standpoints, having salvation in view."

Would you explain that last phrase "having salvation in view"?

It's a qualification that Vatican II makes in its document on Revelation. While deliberately avoiding the word "inerrancy," the Council preferred to state this whole matter of the possibility of errors within the sacred text in this way: " . . . the books of Scripture must be acknowledged as teaching firmly, faithfully, and without error *that truth* which God wanted put into the sacred writings *for the sake of our salvation.*"

Could you give me an example?

The first two chapters of Genesis contain many important religious teachings that touch upon our salvation, that is, that God is the Creator, that what he has created is "good," and that he has given to human beings certain rights and responsibilities toward himself and toward this world he has created. But look at the "scientific" wrappings for these truths: The firmament is a big bronze dome, like an overturned bowl, that keeps back the waters from above. During the act of creation many strange things occur: light appears upon the scene on the first day, but the sources of light — the sun, moon, and stars — are not created until the fourth day. The sun itself is a lamp suspended from the ceiling of the sky.

Any grade-school science student knows that that is not exactly the way Carl Sagan would describe the cosmos. But, despite these scientific errors, we can still say that the biblical author (who could only view the universe as his contemporaries did) wasn't teaching error.

Imagine a NASA scientist coming home from work and telling his toddler son a bedtime story about the cow jumping over the moon. Who would accuse him of teaching incorrect science? He isn't interested in giving his son a course in aerodynamics or in discussing what type of rocket fuel would be needed to put Bossy into lunar orbit. We use our common sense in interpreting his actions and judging his story.

One scholar put it this way: "It is at least irreverent to refuse to approach the Bible with the same respect for its complications that we accord the daily newspaper." That's why Vatican II emphasizes the proper perspective when it says: "For the correct understanding of what the sacred author wanted to assert, due attention must be paid to the customary and characteristic styles of perceiving, speaking, and narrating which prevailed at the time of the sacred writer." So the sacred author made some scientific errors — what difference does that make? He wasn't interested in teaching astronomy or astrophysics; he had more important truths to convey — truths about God himself and about the kinds of relationships we human beings should have with our Creator and with all of creation.

However imperfect the human language in which the Bible is written, it is nonetheless the Word of God in the fullest sense of that term. Only a lively faith will give us a proper appreciation of that. Pray with Psalm 95 "that today you would hear his voice."

6. A Different Kind of History

Basically, your answer in the previous chapter covered only *scientific* errors. I can accept your statement that the biblical authors were not trying to teach the physical sciences. But what about history? And aren't there historical errors in the Bible?

That's a good point. Scientific knowledge may not be essential for the faith of Christians, but history is. Judaism and Christianity are based on certain historical events — the Exodus from Egypt and the life, death, and Resurrection of Jesus. If these central events never actually happened, then we've been living in a dream world. When we say our faith is based on these events actually taking place, what we mean is that there is historical truth at the core of these biblical accounts. We aren't saying that all of the reported details happened exactly that way or that the literary forms used are like those employed by modern historians.

So now you're going to tell me they wrote history differently way back then?

Yes, I am. Our modern historical approach is relatively new. Professional historians today try to get at the bare facts of the past event, stripped of particular points of view. Their impossible dream is: If only we had had video cameras there — with Caesar's conquering legions or at Napoleon's Waterloo — then we could present history as it was! There were no professional historians (in the precise modern sense) in biblical times. But there was a sense of history. Actually, it was much better than ours. Each tribe and kingdom had its storyteller and archivist who recounted the glorious past. The people themselves were committed to this history, which not only told them of their origins but defined them as a nation and gave them a purpose.

But just how truthful is that other way of writing history? Isn't that the point?

Well, let's see. I don't know if you're married, but let's say you are and I asked you to tell me about your wife. You began with a number of external details, her height, hair color, etc. Then you showed me a snapshot and pointed out other features. After awhile you described some events from her childhood, what her family was like, how you first met her, what she's involved with now, her likes and dislikes, interests, and so forth. Let's say after you finished I said to you: "You've done a very good job of describing your wife. Now I know the whole truth about who she is. I feel I understand her as well as you do." What would be your reaction? I'll bet it would be something like this: "There's no way you could know my wife as she really is. There are a thousand other things I could tell you about her; there are a thousand more that I couldn't tell you because you wouldn't understand them. The only way you could know my wife as I do would be to be me and to love her as I do."

Suppose there had been video cameras at the Exodus or in Bethlehem's stable or on the rock of Calvary. Suppose we had these videotapes but *not the Scriptures* — what would we have? Certainly many details that we don't have now: what the temperature was that first Christmas night; what kind of clothes Mary and Joseph wore; what the cave-stable where Jesus was born was really like; how many shepherds came to visit the newborn Child; and similar items of interest. As interesting as all these particulars might be, they would still remain only external details. We would know only what our senses told us about the situation and the specifics of the event. But since we wouldn't have an inkling as to the real meaning and significance of all that happened, why would the details have more than peripheral interest for us? Or let's ask what the viewers of a Calvary videotape would come away with. Basically, they would see a condemned criminal experiencing Roman justice. Is that what Jesus' death means?

Perhaps now we are beginning to realize what a treasure we have in the Bible. The sacred authors have given us not just the central historical truth of these saving events but also the *Spirit-inspired interpretation of them*. Your knowledge of your wife is so rich because it is shot through and through with your love of her. Our scriptural knowledge of God and his Son is so rich because it is shot through and through with the loving faith of the biblical authors and their communities. Let's be forever grateful for this "pearl of great price" that God has put into our hands: our holy Bible.

7. A Record of Growth

You've taken care of my problems concerning scientific and historical errors in the Bible so well that I'm encouraged to ask a question that some of my friends have told me is wrong even to mention. Could an inspired author make a genuine mistake *in a matter pertaining to religious belief?* In other words, does the Bible ever teach *incorrect doctrine* about God, about our relationship to him, and about how he wants us to live?

Get ready for a surprise. I don't feel that it's wrong to ask questions such as yours — that it doesn't show proper respect for God's Word. I cannot agree with that.

Why?

Because there are many devout, sincere lovers of the Bible who are troubled at having come across some passage or part of the Bible which just doesn't seem to fit with everything else they believe.

Would you mention a few of the disturbing things a Bible reader could encounter? That way I'll be ready for them.

Sure. Suppose a person familiar with Isaiah 2:4 — " . . . They shall beat their swords into ploughshares, and their spears into pruning hooks" — comes across this text in Joel, "Beat your ploughshares into swords, and your pruning hooks into spears..." (Joel 4:10). Since God is the author of the whole Bible, how could one part say exactly the opposite of another part?

And there are other problems related to the treatment of war. The Hebrew word for war, *milhamah,* occurs more than three hundred times in the Old Testament. Many people find it disturbing to read the ruthless laws of war in Deuteronomy 20:10-18, and even more to see how these laws were carried out as described in Joshua or Judges. Can we really believe that the wholesale slaughter of men, women, and children actually was commanded by God? How can we reconcile this conception of God with the New Testament description of God as a loving father?

Some even run into problems concerning immortality and the Final Judgment. Many scholars believe that Job 14:13-22 and Sirach 14:16-17, 17:22-23, 38:21 deny an afterlife. It's not that these authors were ignorant of the possibility of an afterlife; they brought it up and then rejected it. How does one reconcile the Word of God in Job or Sirach that seems contradictory to the Word of God taught by Jesus himself?

And how would you interpret " . . . we who live, who survive until his coming . . . " (1 Thessalonians 4:15)? It certainly sounds like Paul expected to be alive at the Second Coming of Jesus. Was this an error on the great apostle's part?

Our response begins with two quotes from Vatican II: " . . . the books of Scripture must be acknowledged as teaching firmly, faithfully, and without error that truth which God wanted put into the sacred writings for the sake of our salvation" (Dogmatic Constitution on Divine Revelation, #11).

" . . . the words of God, expressed in human language, have been made like human discourse, just as of old the Word of the eternal Father, when he took to Himself the weak flesh of humanity, became like other men" (Dogmatic Constitution on Divine Revelation, #13). Just as Jesus emptied himself in taking on our human nature, so God's words in the Bible empty themselves, that is, they become limited, time-conditioned, and somewhat inadequate to the realities to which they point.

Three other considerations: (1) Many apparent "errors" vanish when we see how they are part of a particular literary form. The truth of a poem, epic, parable, or some other literary type is different but *just as valid* as the truth of a factual documentary or a scientific treatise. (2) In the Gospels we can note the disciples' developing faith. As they became more familiar with the Master, their commitment deepened. But at the end of his life Jesus commented that even then they were not capable of grasping everything. This understanding would come only with the arrival of the Holy Spirit. Similarly, in Old Testament times, though spread out over centuries, many doctrines and ethical teachings underwent gradual development: belief in one God, in an afterlife, in monogamy, and so forth. The Bible preserves not only the Word of God but the response to and gradual assimilation of it, in faith, by the People of God. (3) Everything must be taken in context — the verse in the context of the paragraph, the paragraph in the context of the particular chapter and book, the book in the context of the whole Bible, Old and New Testaments, and, finally and of great importance for the way we lead our lives, the Bible itself must be viewed in the context of the community's sustaining faith. Only in this way will we be able to grasp that "truth which God wanted put into the sacred writings *for the sake of our salvation.*"

8. Those "Missing Books"

Our Bible study group ran into something that really puzzled us: our Bibles are different! Some of us couldn't find some of the books at all. Would you please explain how this could happen.

Your study group must have been using both Protestant and Catholic Bibles. Most of the time this would cause no problem, but sooner or later there would be some confusion.

But why are there two different versions of God's Word?

Let me begin by defining a term: canon. Originally, this was a Greek word which meant a measuring stick or a boundary. When referring to the Bible, it means the official list of books that "measure up" and, therefore, are within the Bible. Only these books on this list are recognized as being truly *inspired*.

It so happened that down through the ages the status of several books of the Old Testament had been questioned. At various times and places, some Jewish and some Christian communities vouched for them, and some didn't. The result was a mess: we ended up with two canons, one longer than the other. So now Catholics accept forty-six books as canonical, while many Protestants accept only thirty-nine. The disputed books are: Tobit, Judith, Wisdom, Sirach, Baruch, 1 and 2 Maccabees, and some sections of Esther and Daniel. Protestants call these the *apocryphal* books and put them in a separate section in their Bible. Because Catholics consider these same books fully inspired they call them *deuterocanonical* and place them right along with the other books. If that wasn't confusion enough, we have another terminology mixup to unscramble. You see, there exists another whole collection of ancient Jewish writings which bear some superficial resemblance to the Scriptures. Neither Catholics nor Protestants accept them as being inspired by God, as belonging to the Bible. But the trouble is that these noncanonical writings have been tagged with two names, one Protestant, one Catholic. Protestants call them *pseudepigrapha;* while Catholics call them *apocryphal* — that's right, the same term used by Protestants for the books called "deuterocanonical" by Catholics.

So, what's the story behind these two canons?

During the first century A.D. there were two Jewish Bibles recognized as Sacred Scripture (what we have come to call the Old Testament — the New Testament wasn't completed yet). The shorter one, the Hebrew Bible, was best known in Judea and Galilee. The longer Bible, the Septuagint, a translation from Hebrew to Greek, was quite popular among Greek-speaking Jews and Christians everywhere. Although no definite canon had made the official and critical choice between these two versions, church life and practice continued.

At the Council of Trent (1545) the final canon was decided upon for Catholics — the longer Septuagint was embraced. Meanwhile, Luther and other Reformation scholars, in trying to get back to a more primitive Christianity, chose the shorter Hebrew canon. Lacking the tools of modern research, they made a natural mistake; they thought the Hebrew Bible was the version the early Christians favored. But after considering all the evidence, recent scholarship, Catholic and Protestant, now considers this position untenable. So the Catholic bishops at Trent, in accepting the longer canon, had managed to preserve an authentic memory of the earliest days of Christianity.

Through scholarship and ecumenical prayer we are steadily getting closer to the day when all Christians will kneel down together to thank God for the great treasure of his holy Word — in one and the same Bible!

9. The "Old Laws"

Where have the Ten Commandments gone? In the old days, everyone learned them by heart. It was impressed on us at home, at school, and through sermons that we should strive to keep the Ten Commandments in our daily lives. Now we're told that they were meant for the people in the Old Testament but not for us in New Testament times. The argument goes this way: In view of Jesus' "two great commandments of love," why would a Christian need the added burden of these ancient rules made for another time and place? Is any of this true? I must say that I am confused.

The commandments are indeed relevant to Christianity. In fact, Jesus saw these divine guidelines as *indispensable* to anyone seeking Christian perfection:

"Another time a man came up to him and said, 'Teacher, what good must I do to possess everlasting life?' He answered, 'Why do you question me about what is good? There is One who is good. If you wish to enter into life, keep the commandments.' 'Which ones?' he asked. Jesus replied, ' "You shall not kill"; "You shall not commit adultery"; "You shall not steal"; "You shall not bear false witness"; "Honor your father and your mother"; and "Love your neighbor as yourself." ' The young man said to him, 'I have kept all these; what do I need to do further?' Jesus told him, 'If you seek perfection, go, sell your possessions, and give to the poor. You will then have treasure in heaven. Afterward, come back and follow me.' Hearing these words, the young man went away sad, for his possessions were many" (Matthew 19:16-22).

So, no one can write off the Ten Commandments as belonging to the Old Testament and as irrelevant to the New. By no means! Otherwise, we would be contradicting Jesus, who said: "Do not think that I have come to abolish the law and the prophets. I have come, not to abolish them, but to fulfill them" (Matthew 5:17).

Perhaps, instead of asking, "Where have the Ten Commandments gone?" I should ask, "Where did they come from?" If they are relevant to all times and places, however different their lifestyles, what was their historical origin?

The ratifying of the Covenant pact on Mount Sinai was the setting for the commandments. God had selected the Israelites as "his people." They had just experienced, marvelously, what the liberating power of their God could do. They had been slaves for a long time, and now they were free. The terms of their new relationship with God — what it meant to be his people — were summed up in the Decalogue, the "ten sayings," of Yahweh. In one package, the Israelites were given precise, definite, and comprehensive guidelines to help them live up to their new dignity. Good Israelites then and good Jews now greatly appreciate this. These laws are not seen as burdens laid on from on high. They are viewed in the context of the loving relationship between God and his people. Their attitude can be compared to that of children toward the rules made by parents for their protection and happiness.

I just cannot see how adults and, much less, children could actually welcome rules.

Maybe a story will help. I'm reminded of a thirteen-year-old girl whose parents were very permissive. They never refused her anything. They let her make her own decisions and set her own limits. One night she decided to test the whole relationship. Though it scared her, she deliberately stayed out all night — she wanted to see what her parents would do; would they punish her? What really happened was that they didn't even notice. She was crushed. Even at her young age, she interpreted the permissiveness of her parents as a sign that they didn't care enough about her to give her some rules to live by.

In much the same way, the Israelites and Jews today see the commandments as a sign of God's protection and care.

We Christians are the "People of God" of the New Covenant. Our religious experience is quite different from the ancient Israelites. Jesus Christ, the Promised One, has come. He lived among us, was put to death, and, now risen, again lives among us. Our morality must be based primarily on a life of love for God and our fellow human beings, in union with Christ.

But how can we be sure that our life of love is real and not just a matter of words and feelings?

We can compare it to the definition of love of God and love of humankind given us in the Ten Commandments. But we must go beyond what is explicitly stated there. If anything, it emphasizes its importance since this is where a Christian *begins*.

Jesus insisted that even the least significant of the commandments should be kept by his disciples. But immediately after this urging, Jesus demands more of his followers.

He does this especially in his famous Sermon on the Mount (see Matthew 5, 6, and 7). There, and in other places, you will notice an extremely important dimension to Christian moral teaching. In stark contrast to the morality of some Pharisees, Jesus taught a "morality of the heart." To our Lord, the internal motive from which an action springs is more important than the external act itself. For example, notice the different levels involved in the movement from the external commandments to the deepest recesses of the heart: First, we must not *murder* or *injure* anyone. We must not *curse* them or destroy their reputations with our *tongues*. We must not even *think hateful thoughts* about them. In fact, we must go beyond all this by *forgiving* and even *loving* those who injure us.

This is what leading a Christian life means — it involves the heart and will in ever-deeper commitments. But the starting point is *always* the Ten Commandments. They cannot be brushed aside without the gravest consequences. Only after keeping them to the best of our abilities can we, with the young man who was considering becoming a follower of Christ, ask: "What do I need to do further?"

10. The "Boring" Parts

The Old Testament just doesn't appeal to me. I guess I feel that when Christ came the New Testament replaced the Old. . . . So why bother with ancient prophecies that have already come true?

I'm glad you're so open about the way you feel, but I'm afraid that it has made you treat the Old Testament as though Jesus came to do away with it. That isn't what he intended. Listen to the words of Jesus: "Do not think that I have come to abolish the law and the prophets. I have come, not to abolish them, but to fulfill them" (Matthew 5:17).

Could you give me some idea of what I could personally get out of reading the Old Testament?

Yes. For one thing, the Old Testament would help you to understand the New. Jesus Christ was born into and lived in a culture that was religious through and through. A devout Jew scarcely had a thought that was not somehow connected with the often-told story of how God had saved his people and what that divine action promised for the future. Of course, the primary vehicle for these remembrances was Sacred Scripture itself. This, at the time, was the Old Testament. Jesus no doubt knew a large part of the inspired text by heart. Religious ideas, symbols, and values that barely impress us were bursting with meaning for him. Run down a list of words and try to imagine what would have gone on in Jesus' heart and mind (compared to ours) on hearing these words: slavery, Passover, Exodus, covenant, Chosen People, temple, sacrifice, scapegoat, Son of Man, prophet, exile, Messiah, sin, life, death, Kingdom of God. Immersing ourselves in the Old Testament will not close the gap completely, but at least it will put us in touch with the rich religious heritage which we share with Jesus.

OK. So the Old Testament will help me understand the New. But it doesn't say anything to everyday life today, does it?

Yes, it does. The Old Testament was born out of human struggle, and is a reflection of human life at its deepest. By reflecting on the major stories and themes of the Old Testament, fundamental elements of our own lives can be evoked and made part of our prayer. With Job we can question why innocent people suffer; with Qoheleth we can discern why a life without God is absurd; with the betrothed couple of the Song of Songs we can sing of the joys of young love; with the uncompromising prophets we can demand fidelity to the Law and justice for the disadvantaged; with the psalmist we can cry out for help or fill the heavens with praise and wonder for the mighty works of God. In a word, unchanging human life is being presented in the sacred text. The Old Testament has a facility of establishing resonance with the deepest parts of our humanity. Like a little child in his father's arms, we are held in God's hands.

> Though the mountains leave their place
>   and the hills be shaken,
> My love shall never leave you
>   nor my covenant of peace be shaken,
>   says the LORD . . . (Isaiah 54:10).

That should just about do it. Or does the Old Testament, as the Word of God, have still more to offer?

I believe so. The Old Testament can help us prepare for the Second Coming as no other book can. The patriarchs, prophets, and faithful of the Old Testament longed for the establishment of God's Kingdom. They believed that when the Messiah came all evil, injustice, suffering, and even death would be overcome. Jesus was this long-awaited Messiah, but sin and suffering still exist. Christ did indeed inaugurate the Kingdom of God, establishing the New Covenant in his blood, but he wanted his disciples to cooperate with him in building up this Kingdom throughout the world. So, he bequeathed his own Spirit to the new People of God to guide and strengthen them in their work. Caught up in the day-to-day struggle, we can sometimes forget that victory is on the horizon, that there will be a Second Coming of Christ. Frequent recourse to the Old Testament can sharpen our longing for that day. And what a day it will be! The promise contained in the ancient covenant will, indeed, be fulfilled, but in ways exceeding even the wildest dreams of the Old Testament authors.

It would be a shame to miss out on the treasures of the Old Testament, wouldn't it? Start reading it today!

11. "Yahweh" and "Jehovah"

Some songs in our new parish hymnal refer to God as "Yahweh." Is this what the Jews used to call God? Is there anything about it in the Bible?

Yes, there's quite a bit about that expression, "Yahweh," in the Bible. In fact, that strange-looking word is at the very heart of one of the most mysterious stories in the Book of Exodus:

"But," said Moses to God, "when I go to the Israelites and say to them, 'The God of your fathers has sent me to you,' if they ask me, 'What is his name?' what am I to tell them?" God replied, "I am who am" . . . (Exodus 3:13-14).

I don't see what you are getting at. "Yahweh" doesn't show up in those verses at all.

That's true. Not in this English translation. But if we had read them in the Hebrew, the four Hebrew consonants which are the equivalents of our Y, H, W and H would have been where the "I am who am" is. That whole phrase replaces those four letters.

How would a rabbi or scholar pronounce that?

A devout Jew reading the Scriptures wouldn't pronounce those letters at all. But today's scholars have more or less agreed on the pronunciation Yahweh (yă we), with the *a* as in "car" and the *e* as in "ten," but this is really only an educated guess.

Why wouldn't a devout Jew pronounce them?

Because pious Jews from time immemorial have not considered their tongues worthy to utter out loud the proper personal name of God himself.

So what did they do when they came to the four letters?

Instead of saying God's name, they used, and still do, his title "Lord," which is *Adonai* in Hebrew. To remind themselves to say "Adonai," the vowels *a, o, a* are put under the consonants *Y, H, W, H,* which are passed over in silent respect. Centuries ago, someone misunderstood all this and interjected the *a, o, a* of Adonai between the four sacred consonants, thereby producing the nonbiblical hybrid "YaHoWaH" which later became the Jehovah of many old English Bibles.

But does this most sacred name mean something, or is it just a name like Mary or John?

Just a minute! John and Mary are very meaningful names. Because they, like many of our more common names, have their origins in languages no longer spoken, they no longer say anything significant to us. But those names originally made strong statements about the persons who bore them. It spoke of the person's origins, traits, destiny, or personality. All this was especially true with the people of Old Testament times. *Mary* means "exalted one"; *John* means "God has shown favor."

Then I would presume that "Yahweh" has a profound meaning.

You're right. There is general agreement that the word is derived from the archaic form of the verb "to be." Scholar W. F. Albright proposes that it is only the first part of a longer word which means: "He brings into being whatever comes into being." The name therefore designates God as Creator of the universe, the Source of all life. Another scholar, J. F. McKenzie, emphasizes the same point: "Perhaps no word better sums up the biblical conception of Yahweh than the word 'living'; for the life of Yahweh includes his personal reality, his activity and his will, his nearness joined with his utter transcendence over man, over creation, over all beings." God is the absolute and necessary Being, containing in himself the fullness of all being, life, and love. Our life came from God, and we remain in existence because he holds us in his loving hand. Saint Paul seems to echo this when he says, "In him we live and move and have our being . . ." (Acts 17:28).

Fortunately, we do not have to depend on the meaning of God's name as given to Moses for all that we can know about God. The Letter to the Hebrews makes this point very well:

In times past, God spoke in fragmentary and varied ways to our fathers through the prophets; in this, the final age, he has spoken to us through his Son, whom he has made heir of all things and through whom he first created the universe. This Son is the reflection of the Father's glory, the exact representation of the Father's being, and he sustains all things by his powerful word . . . (Hebrews 1:1-3).

The best way, then, to learn what Yahweh means is to go to the Word-made-flesh, Jesus Christ. When we do that we will get to know God in the highly personal way that Jesus hoped that we would when he suggested that we address God as "Father."

12. Scandalous Violence

For the first time in my life, I have been reading the Bible seriously and trying to understand it. I was going along fine until I ran into some passages where God seems to be advocating violence — even the wholesale slaughter of people, including women and children. How can I reconcile this with my idea of God as a loving father?

You have brought up a point that has challenged Bible readers for centuries. It's not a small matter. The concept a person has of God — whether he is a thunderbolt-throwing, vengeful despot; a loving father; or something in-between — affects every aspect of a person's life.

I think it best to start with very simple basics. You'll remember that we tried to sort out various kinds of things that scriptural writers just happened to do and to keep them separate from what they did as their primary concern. In other words, we tried to distinguish between incidentals and what was really essential. Thus we saw that biblical writers recorded the limited astronomical views of their time, but they did so to teach in God's name that these wonders (that they so poorly understood) had God as their source. Their theology was great; their astronomy was poor.

Something a bit more complicated than that takes place in the stories of Israel's bloody wars in the Promised Land. They are, at one and the same time, recording the *history* of Israel's moral and religious development in response to God's revelation, *and* they are *proclaiming God's revealed will* for Israel and for humankind.

We and Jews today, as Israel did then, *believe* that God called Israel to be as different from other nations as he himself was from the "gods" that gave expression to the ideals of other nations. We believe that this was God's will for Israel and for humankind.

So God called Israel to be different from other peoples, and yet Israel was as bloody as the other nations. And you say this has a lesson for us?

You'll have to slow down a bit to get my point. The "historical" books of the Old Testament record more than this special calling. In the manner of the time, they record, as well, Israel's response to this call. As such it is the story of a gradual development in moral sensitivity and of a transformation.

The religious history of Israel starts with a people accepting the challenge to be different — to lift themselves above the insensitive lack of love that surrounded them in a cruel, primitive world. But when Israel learned from humiliating experience that it could not be faithful to its call if cohabiting with a people whose life-style constantly lured it back to the old ways, it jumped to this conclusion: The God who willed this new way of life must also will as well the destruction of all that made it humanly impossible.

Did they really believe this or merely use it as an excuse?

The evidence indicates that Israel came to this conclusion much against its own inclination. Certainly, its writers presented this implied command as coming directly from God. (The same writers presented the *details* of the worship commanded in the Decalogue as coming *directly* from God.) *MOSES — GOD'S MESSENGER*

So they honestly believed this was God's will. But what's the point for us?

Both early and later books of the Bible, while recounting these religious wars, point out how the faithfulness of Israel was tested in its efforts to comply with the dictates of what it judged to be God's implied will for it. (Remember how we discussed studying all parts of the Bible in relation to the whole!)

The immediate *religious lesson,* as distinct from the religious history involved, then, is concerned with *faithfulness to the will of God as understood* — not with the violent solution to a social problem.

At the same time, from the perspective of the New Testament, we can see that these ancient Israelites, by following their own convictions, however abhorrent to us, made possible a way of life that would nurture a sensitivity that would ultimately reject this whole violent way of dealing with social problems.

These stories, then, tell us a great deal about the religion of Israel at the time. Secular historians of religion would find them interesting as such. But that is not our concern. What we care about is that these stories, as the Word of God, *reveal* for all time *a patient Father* working with his children who were and are so slow to grasp the light!

To sum it all up, if there's one thing we can be certain of in our reading of the Scriptures, it is this — if at any time any passage seems to make God a cruel tyrant, our interpretation has to be incorrect. It simply doesn't fit with everything else the Scriptures say of him. It doesn't match the idea of God expressed over and over in the Old and New Testaments: God is a loving Father. Finally, if you really want to know what God is like, look to Jesus: "He is the image of the invisible God . . . " (Colossians 1:15).

13. The Word on Abortion

The following appeared recently in the letter section of a nationally syndicated column: "I believe abortion is not wrong, according to the Bible. Matthew says: 'Better to lose part of your body than to have it all cast into Gehenna' (Matthew 5:29)." Are these verses in fact supportive of a pro-abortion stance?

The proponents of abortion insist upon calling the unborn infant "the fetus" to reduce the impact that would result from our use of ordinary language to describe what they advocate, "killing a baby." They also refer to the same child as a "part of the (mother's) body" to enhance the claims of the pregnant woman to having her rights considered to the exclusion of the rights of the infant within her. This terminology is of very recent origin and has no scientific validity. Nor does it have anything to do with the phrase found in *The New American Bible* translation of Matthew 5:29 quoted above.

Does the Bible give any explicit condemnation of abortion?

Not in so many "Thou shalt not" words. However, it does offer us several implicit references to this evil practice. More impressive, however, than a collection of individual specific texts is the pervasive, ever-present aura of respect that the Scriptures place around life. If there is one clear teaching in the Bible, it is that God is the Author of all life.

The ancient Jews were surrounded by pagan societies in which both abortion and infanticide were widely practiced and routinely accepted. But the Israelite nation abhorred these unnatural practices. They were completely alien to the basic assumptions that undergirded the Jewish orientation to life: first, their God-inspired duty to populate the earth as the Chosen People from whom, at the appointed time, the Messiah would come; second, a deep sense of the sanctity of life as God's special gift.

Would you give a few Old Testament references that touch upon this matter of abortion or spotlight the Jewish respect for life in the womb?

Exodus 21:22-25 begins with, "When men have a fight and hurt a pregnant woman. . . ." Jewish commentators disputed about various words in these verses; but, far from considering abortion as either meant or implied in the text, they were in agreement that human beings are not allowed to infringe upon God's complete sovereignty over life in the womb. In describing the fierceness of the Medes, the prophet Isaiah says that they are so terrible that they even violate this protected territory:

> The fruit of the womb they shall not spare,
> nor shall they have eyes of pity for children (Isaiah 13:18).

Atrocity against the unborn is regarded as even more serious than that perpetrated against the mother. To deny the human being even the right to be born is regarded as the height of barbarity.

But do the Scriptures actually treat unborn infants as human beings with personalities of their own or as parts of their mothers?

God's view of the unborn seems to be made overwhelmingly clear in the Scriptures. The psalmist says to God, "you knit me in my mother's womb" (see Psalm 139:13). The Lord addresses Jeremiah:

> Before I formed you in the womb I knew you,
> before you were born I dedicated you . . ." (see Jeremiah 1:5).

The mother of the Maccabees encourages her seven sons with the words:

> I do not know how you came into existence in my womb; it was not I who gave you the breath of life . . . (2 Maccabees 7:22).

The attitude expressed in the New Testament is even clearer, and respect for the personalities of the unborn is highly enhanced. At a very early point in the unfolding story of God's Son become incarnate in Mary's womb, the focus shifts to the personalities of the unborn. Shortly after Jesus' conception, Mary visits her cousin Elizabeth, who is also pregnant with a son — John the Baptizer.

And in Luke's words: "When Elizabeth heard Mary's greeting, the baby leapt in her womb . . . " (Luke 1:41) — a highly personal reaction of an infant in his sixth month to his cousin and Lord, still in his first month and deep within his Mother!

Every page of the Bible proclaims God as Lord of the living — no, more than that — as a doting parent who has a special, unexplainable predilection for us human beings.

> Can a mother forget her infant,
>> be without tenderness for the child of her womb?
> Even should she forget,
>> I will never forget you (Isaiah 49:15).

14. The Gospels and the Risen Christ

Recently, I heard a priest make a statement I didn't quite understand. He said: "The Church didn't spring up from the Gospels; rather, it was the other way around — the Gospels sprang up in the Church." Can you shed any light on what he meant?

The priest was probably talking about how the Gospels came into being and took shape within the early Christian communities. They didn't just appear on the scene, full-blown, shortly after the Lord's Ascension. It took at least thirty-five years before the first Gospel was written, and those intervening decades weren't periods of inactivity. We now know our New Testament text is the end result of a living process, a three-stage process which left its mark on the final documents. While not immediately evident, these stages or levels can still be discerned in the sacred texts.

I'd appreciate it if you would start at the earliest stage and go slow — this is new to me.

At the first stage, there was an urgent concern to preserve the words and actions of Jesus during the course of his earthly ministry. Materials from this stage cover the time span from Jesus' birth (probably about 5 or 4 B.C.) until his death (around A.D. 30). Here we hear his preaching about God, about the Kingdom, and about himself — usually in the form of very pointed stories called parables — parables which profoundly challenged his audience.

So, then, the evangelists could begin their work in the second stage, right?

No, not so fast. If by "their work" you mean the actual composing (writing, editing, and organizing) of the Gospels, no, it couldn't begin yet. They didn't have all the materials that were to go into them.

So, what did they need besides the words and actions of Jesus?

The fruits of the faith of the early Christian community, how it began to view Christ in the period following Pentecost — that is, from about A.D. 30 to about 65 or 70. Though some written material stems from this time (a collection of Jesus' sayings, lists of miracles, perhaps accounts of the Passion, etc.), this is mostly about what the early Church felt, thought, and witnessed to in their preaching about the "Lord Jesus." After all, the One they had walked with and talked with, their beloved Master, who had died a terrible death as a condemned criminal — this very same One they now encountered alive, risen, glorified! From this time on, whenever they spoke of Jesus' words and deeds (Stage One material), they would feel impelled to proclaim at the same time their "Resurrection faith." We could say that Stage Two material sees everything through "Easter glasses."

Are you saying that stage two faith affected even first stage materials like the parables?

Exactly. Let's take a look at what was happening already, early in this second stage, to the retelling of Jesus' parables. These intriguing stories, which had been used by the Lord to challenge his listeners' basic assumptions, were now seen as one of the principal ways of proclaiming the "Good News" to a brand new audience, one that was largely non-Jewish, spoke a different language, and belonged to a different culture. Naturally, the preacher felt that certain adaptations and explanations were necessary if he was going to get his point across.

Nor were things sitting still for the young Christian communities. They, too, were experiencing new situations, facing problems that had not existed during Jesus' lifetime. That's why the preacher, guided by the Spirit (Jesus' gift to his community), didn't hesitate to invest the original core parables with new meanings and new applications. In this way he could continue using these parables not just as ways of recalling Jesus' life and preaching but also as a way of comforting and confronting his fellow believers at the present. In this way Jesus' basic challenge was kept alive.

So, finally, in Stage Three we arrive at the time of the *actual writing of the Gospels* by Matthew, Mark, Luke, and John?

Yes. But, strictly speaking, Mark's name should be first because his Gospel, written either in A.D. 65 or 70, was first to appear. Matthew's and Luke's were next, both around 80 or 85. Finally, John's unique Gospel graced the scene around 90 or 95. Pursuing a goal peculiar to each, and adapting to their own situations, the evangelists made extensive use of the community's faith understanding of Jesus (in other words, the oral and written material of Stage Two). But, in putting pen to papyrus, the Gospel writers didn't just transcribe all this material like a secretary might be asked to do. To say the least, they did some very creative compiling and editing. They *selected* from this rich tradition (the remembered sayings, parables, miracle stories, etc.), *wove these together* into their own literary compositions, and *fashioned* all this into the unique literary form that we call "gospel," indeed, into our four Gospels, the most precious gems of God's revelation.

I think I get what you mean. But could you, perhaps by using the parables, give me some sense of the entire process?

I'll try. For many people, the Good Shepherd carrying the lamb in his arms is a favorite portrayal of Christ. Obviously, this image came from the parable of the lost sheep, as recounted by Luke (Luke 15:3-7). Matthew also tells the same tale (Matthew 18:12-14). Let's compare the two versions and see how they differ. Most experts think that Luke's verses 3 to 6 are closest to the original. (The moral, verse 7, was added later, either by the early Church or by Luke himself.) In his account, Luke has Jesus addressing this parable to the Pharisees and other religious leaders, who felt his association with sinners was inexcusable. What does Jesus want to say to his critics? As one renowned scholar put it: "Jesus asserted that, just as a shepherd rejoices over the lost sheep he has found, so God rejoices over the repentant sinner. He rejoices because he can forgive. That, says Jesus, is why I receive sinners."

Matthew's account, on the other hand, has Jesus speaking to a different audience, a much friendlier one — his own disciples — rather than the critical Pharisees. Naturally, then, the moral, verse 14 (added either by the early Church or by Matthew) reflects a different emphasis. The parable now says: You should take care of the "least members" of your community. You should go after your fallen-aways as persistently as the shepherd seeks the stray sheep. The basic parable (which, in Luke's version, was an apologia for Jesus' way of seeking out sinners) has now become a call to the leaders of the community to exercise faithful pastorship toward their own, especially those weak in faith.

That makes it a lot clearer. Could I ask for just one more example?

The case of the parable of the sower is a little more complicated. It appears in three of the Gospels: Matthew 13:3-9; Mark 4:3-9; Luke 8:5-8. Though it's difficult to reconstruct the original form of the parable, the meaning Jesus intended is fairly obvious. He told a story about a farmer who sows a few handfuls of seed and, despite all the agricultural vicissitudes of that time and place, gathers in many bushels of grain. He enjoys a highly successful harvest! In other words, despite what seem to be frustrations and failures, Jesus' ministry will certainly bear fruit, and in a manner exceeding all expectations. The original parable was meant, then, as encouragement for his disciples and as an invitation for them to trust the Father just as Jesus did.

That the early Church and/or the evangelists have a different interpretation can be seen by reading the following verses: Matthew 13:18-23; Mark 4:14-20; Luke 8:11-15. The simple proclamation-of-hope story told by Jesus (Stage One) has been extended and allegorized by the preacher (Stage Two) and/or the evangelist (Stage Three) to become a kind of warning, an elaborate exhortation to the Christian community. Was this legitimate? Yes. The times demanded that the people be reminded that it wasn't sufficient merely to hear the Word — they must also act in such a way that they bear fruit. Do we need to hear the same message today (and also the original message)? If we look into our hearts we have the answer.

Could you summarize what you've been saying about what makes the Gospels unique?

The Gospels cast light on the ministry of Jesus (stage one), on subsequent concerns of the early Church (stage two), and, especially, on the view of Christ held by the evangelist as he instructed a Christian community several generations after Jesus (stage three). But, notice, there's something missing.

Something missing in the Gospels?

Yes, you won't find a trace of nostalgia in any of them. Perhaps we can understand why there isn't if we recall that for the early Christians *Jesus was not really gone* — he was still with them in his Spirit. What this sense of the living Lord's presence meant, practically, we have just seen in the freedom with which the Church modified the various parables. If the preachers of stage two and the evangelists of stage three had merely repeated Jesus' parables (retelling them exactly, word for word), they would have limited them to being learned answers to *past* problems. Adapting the parables to new Church situations not envisaged by Jesus enabled the preachers and evangelists to once again challenge current Christian ways of thinking and acting. This was necessary because, in some areas, the religious thought patterns and attitudes of the early Church were in danger of becoming just as fixed as those that Jesus had confronted in, for example, the rigid mentality of the Pharisees.

But this brings up a new question which I hope you won't find disrespectful. Why stop at the stage of adaptation of the parables reached when the evangelist wrote?

There's no good reason to do so. If we did, we would again be limiting the parables to being learned answers to *past* problems, except that now the past is the time of the evangelists in the last third of the first century instead of Jesus' time in the first third. We urgently need to discover how the parables (and, in fact, the whole gospel and the entire Bible) can challenge *us* now with *our* fixed religious views.

That's why the error in a naïve, fundamentalist view of the Gospels can be seen as precisely this: the confusing of stage three with stage one. Such a simplistic approach — which totally ignores the critical role of the early Church in the Gospels' formation — could well lead to a misinterpretation of God's Word, despite good intentions all around.

But does this mean that we can't read the Gospels or the rest of the Bible unless we become scholars?

By no means! We can feel perfectly secure as long as we try to "think with the Church." The Holy Spirit will protect us from misuse of the inspired text because we are dwelling within the Christian community — that community where the Gospels originated and whose principal work is to proclaim the "good news" that Jesus is Lord!

15. The Good News in Four Versions

I've noticed that sometimes the Gospels are a lot alike and sometimes they're quite different. Is this because the evangelists copied a great deal from each other but sometimes changed things?

It's true that much of the basic material is similar in the first three Gospels. (The Fourth Gospel, John's, has its own unique style and approach.) It's also true that while Matthew and Luke copied extensively from Mark (the oldest Gospel), they didn't hesitate to change things when it suited them, retelling the stories to fit their own purposes and, also, adding material from other sources.

I don't want to go into all the details right here. But could you somehow give me some sense of the principal differences among the Gospels?

The account of the Passion is a good place to begin. Each of the evangelists tells the story of Jesus' suffering and death in his own unique way.

So, you'll begin with Mark, of course.

Yes. Mark's, the first Gospel, was intended for Gentile Christian readers or, at least, for readers unfamiliar with Jewish customs. His style is direct and serious. He lets the facts speak for themselves without trying to embellish them. That's why he sometimes sounds rather harsh — almost like he is trying to upset us. For example, the story of the Last Supper is framed by the intimation of two ominous events: Judas' betrayal and Peter's denial. Mark is telling us that Jesus knows what is to come; he is the one who directs his Passion. At this final meal he offers up his Body and Blood for humankind, including his disciples, knowing full well that most of those present will not be faithful during the approaching ordeal. Mark describes Jesus in the Garden of Gethsemane as experiencing great anguish, prostrate with the fear of his approaching death. When Judas appears, accompanied by a crowd with swords and clubs, and the Master is about to be arrested, all of his disciples forsake him, even the young man who starts to follow him but then flees, naked. (This youth may have been the evangelist himself; some scholars think so.) At his trial, standing before Pilate, Jesus claims to be king, while at the same time the high priests incite the crowd to shout "Crucify him!" Finally, Christ dies on the Cross, abandoned by all, apparently even by the Father. But the evangelist has the Gentile soldier acknowledge that "Clearly this man was the Son of God!" Mark's purpose in writing his Gospel was precisely to lead the reader to make that same profession of faith.

How much of that could Matthew really change?

Let's see. Matthew wrote for Christians of Jewish origin. Such a group would know the Scriptures very well. That's why the evangelist referred to more than 130 Old Testament passages. He was pointing out how certain events in Jesus' life fulfilled what their treasured Scriptures had said about the Messiah. But, if that is so, how could the Jewish religious leaders, whose all-important task it was to understand the Scriptures and, thereby, to recognize this Messiah when he came, actually end up condemning Jesus? Matthew says it was because these leaders had become identified with those princes of Psalm 2 who "conspire together against the LORD and against his anointed."

Using the teaching methods of a rabbi, Matthew sometimes brings together several passages in a subtle way to produce a quotation which suits him. Thus he combined Zechariah 11:12 and Jeremiah 18:2 to explain the death of Judas. Similarly, Matthew indicates that Judas' betrayal, tragic as it was, also fulfilled the Scriptures. In Zechariah 11:13, the people rejected God and, to mock him, paid him the price of a slave, thirty pieces of silver. In Jesus, then, it is God himself who is being sold. For Matthew, Christ's death marks the end of the old world and the beginning of the new, thereby fulfilling the Scriptures.

And what about Luke?

For Luke, the whole of the Passion is internalized. In Gethsemane, Jesus' inner struggle forced blood through his pores. But, having committed himself completely to his Father's will, he rises and shows his sensitive concern for others. He welcomes Judas gently, heals the servant's ear, speaks to the women who lament his fate, and forgives even his executioners. Finally, Jesus utters a prayer devout Jews say every evening: "Into your hands I commend my spirit," but, significantly, he adds the term, "Father."

Didn't you say that John presents the Passion in an entirely different light?

Yes. For the fourth evangelist the Passion was the triumphal procession of Jesus toward his Father. When he is about to be arrested, Jesus doesn't refer, as he does in Matthew, to legions of angels who could save him; it's enough for him to say, "It is I," and the soldiers fall to the ground. Before Pilate, a dignified Christ is really the judge rather than the one being judged. And, in John's eyes, the lifting up of Jesus on the Cross is also his ascension into glory. "I, when I am lifted up from the earth, will draw all men to me" (12:32). The Cross becomes the throne of glory from which Jesus founds his Church; from his open side flow water and blood, symbolizing the two sacraments of Baptism and the Eucharist.

Yes, the four Gospels differ in many ways, but their basic message — especially in the Passion accounts — is always the same: Jesus loves us and died for us.

16. Those "Lives of Christ"

Whatever happened to the "lives" of Christ? Is it true that modern scholarship doesn't approve of them? I can remember how much they meant to me years ago, and I can't see why they (if they were updated a bit) wouldn't be worthwhile reading nowadays also.

I, too, fondly recall several "lives" of Christ which I read years ago. The ones that come to mind are Fillion's, Ricciotti's, Prat's, and, my favorite, Archbishop Goodier's. While these books are appreciated for the good they did in their day, contemporary Scripture scholars point out that, in light of what is now known about the New Testament, certain problems arise when anyone tries to combine the four Gospels into a "life" or "biography" of Christ. These scholars feel that, despite the genuine piety which inspired these accounts, such "lives" tend to produce the opposite of the intended effect — they actually promote a misreading of the biblical text. In other words, despite good will all around, a somewhat distorted image of Christ sometimes results.

Through no fault of their own, the authors of these old "lives" didn't really understand what a Gospel is. We can tell this by the way they handled the discrepancies that are present in Matthew, Mark, Luke, and John. Since these four Gospels were thought to be straight biographical material, the only thing the authors could do was try to harmonize all these different details and produce one consistent story line. But that meant that the authors had to become literary contortionists. So, that's what they did and, I might add, with considerable ingenuity. By twisting, turning, and rearranging the material over and over, some "Life of Christ" authors felt they could pinpoint precise dates for many of the events in Jesus' life, while others produced maps detailing the exact routes of Jesus' journeys.

Was this focus of interest really so bad?

Perhaps not in itself. But it resulted in their missing much of the theology the sacred authors were trying to get across. What we are saying is: Reconstructing Sacred Scripture in this way ignores the historical and cultural background of the Gospel texts, the perspective of individual authors, and the factors which condition human thinking and language.

Granting all that, what is a person who is sincerely interested in Jesus supposed to do? Are we left to our own resources, or do we have some guidelines from the Holy See in this matter?

Fortunately, we do. Our modern understanding of the Bible began with Pius XII's encyclical of 1943, *Divino afflante Spiritu*

(*Inspired by the Divine Spirit*). In that watershed document the Holy Father strongly insisted on the study of the "literary forms" present in the Bible. He felt that this study would turn out to be one of the major keys to a proper and fruitful interpretation of God's Word. Then in 1964 the Biblical Commission issued *The Instruction Concerning the Historical Truth of the Gospels*. After quoting Pius' encyclical, this instruction took the next step — it espoused outrightly the form-critical and redaction-critical methods of interpretation of the Gospels. At the same time it made explicit mention of the three stages that went into the formation of the canonical Gospels. Finally, The Dogmatic Constitution on Divine Revelation, Vatican II's document on Revelation (1965), summed up what had come before (the 1943 and the 1964 documents), thus making that approach its own official approach with regard to Gospel interpretation.

Modern scholarship has made us even more aware of the all-important purpose of the Gospels: to proclaim that Jesus is Lord. For that we are grateful. We are living in the golden age of biblical studies. Let's mine it for all it's worth!

17. Blaming the Jews

Who was responsible for the death of Jesus? Was it the Jews or the Romans?

The New Testament, which is our primary source of information about the trial and death of Jesus, points an accusing finger at both the Roman authority and the Jewish leadership in Palestine at the time. But what isn't often noticed, it makes this accusation with varying degrees of emphasis, depending on the individual New Testament writers.

For example, when we look at the earliest Passion narrative, that of Mark, the responsibility is shared by the Jewish chief priests, elders, and scribes, and by Pilate. In Matthew's Gospel there seems to be a slight reevaluating of Pilate's role: (1) His wife warns him to have nothing to do "with that holy man" (27:19); (2) Pilate washes his hands and declares: "I am innocent of the blood of this just man . . . " (27:24). Luke continues to shift the blame from the Roman to the Jewish authorities. We find Pilate declaring Jesus innocent not once but three times. At the same time, Luke brings in a very important distinction between the people, on the one hand, and the elders, chief priests, and scribes on the other. Finally, in John's account the trend continues. Besides also declaring Jesus innocent three times, Pilate tries various stratagems to free him. When he finally yields, the evangelist records: "In the end, Pilate handed Jesus over to be crucified" (19:16), and this can only mean that Jesus was handed over to the chief priests and elders. In fact, throughout his Gospel, whenever John says "Jews," he, like Luke, is speaking about the religious leaders and not the ordinary people.

It's very important that when we read these various Passion narratives we always remember that important distinction made originally by Luke (and seconded by John): When the Gospel writers talk about "the Jews," those who persecuted Jesus, they are not referring to *all* Jews. They mean only those few Jewish *leaders* in the time of Jesus who were in conflict with what he preached. At Vatican II, our Catholic bishops made the following official statement about this very matter: "True, authorities of the Jews and those who followed their lead pressed for the death of Christ (cf. Jn. 19:6); still, what happened in His passion cannot be blamed upon all the Jews then living, without distinction, nor upon the Jews of today. Although the Church is the new people of God, the Jews should not be presented as repudiated or cursed by God, as if such views followed from the holy Scriptures. . . . (the Church) deplores the hatred, persecutions, and displays of anti-Semitism directed against the Jews at any time and from any source" (Declaration on the Relationship of the Church to Non-Christian Religions, #4).

A few years ago, the bishops of the United States reaffirmed this teaching of the Council. They pointed out that our official Catholic teaching has "definitely laid to rest this myth (that Jews were and are collectively guilty of the death of Jesus) which has caused so much suffering to the Jewish people. There remains, however, the continuing task of ensuring that nothing which in any way approaches the notion of Jewish collective guilt should be found in any Catholic medium of expression or communication . . . The Jewish people never were, nor are they now, guilty of the death of Christ" (*The Church and the Synagogue*).

How can I be sure that I'm not unconsciously infected with some anti-Semitism?

You might begin by reflecting on another strong statement made by the American bishops in regard to Jews. "Christians have not fully appreciated their Jewish roots. Early in Christian history, it went through a de-Judaizing process that dulled our awareness of our Jewish beginnings. The Jewishness of Jesus, of his mother, his disciples, of the primitive Church was lost from view. That Jesus was called rabbi . . . That he and Peter and Paul worshipped in the temple — these facts were blurred by the controversy that alienated Christians from the synagogue.

"How Jewish the church was toward the midpoint of the first century is dramatically reflected in the description of the 'Council of Jerusalem' (Acts of the Apostles 15). The question at issue was: would Gentile converts to the church have to be circumcised and observe the Mosaic law? The obligation to obey the law was held so firmly by the Jewish Christians of that time that miraculous visions accorded to Peter and Cornelius (Acts of the Apostles 10) were needed to vindicate the contrary contention that Gentile Christians were not so obliged.

"By the third century, however, a de-Judaizing process had set in which tended to undervalue the Jewish origins of the church, a tendency that has surfaced from time to time in devious ways throughout Christian history. Some . . . still convey little appreciation of the Jewishness of that heritage . . . which we derive from Abraham . . . " (*The Church and the Synagogue*).

Reflecting prayerfully on what the bishops have said about the Jews and reading the Old Testament should help. Also, I hope that every time you hear the word "Jew" you will immediately remember that this was the nationality and religion of Jesus and Mary and the apostles. As Pope Pius XI said, we Christians are all "spiritual Semites."

Who was responsible for the death of Jesus? If we look into our hearts we find that the only answer that counts is: our sins have crucified the Lord. But even then, we needn't despair because, according to Luke's Gospel, "Jesus said, 'Father, forgive them; they do not know what they are doing' " (23:34).

18. Jesus' Brothers and Sisters

Did Jesus have any brothers or sisters? I know the Catholic interpretation holds that he didn't. But how do we reconcile this with Scripture (Matthew 12:46, 13:55; Mark 3:31, 6:3; Luke 8:19-21; John 2:12, 7:3-5; Galatians 1:19)?

Let's look at some of the answers that have been given to your question. The first one, espoused by many Protestants, is that the "brothers" and "sisters" in the above texts are, indeed, true siblings of Jesus. This opinion doesn't deny or even question the virginal conception of Jesus in Mary's womb. Rather, it's saying that *after* his birth, Mary and Joseph had marital relations, the fruits of which were younger brothers and sisters for Jesus. Aside from the Catholic objection to this (the tradition of Mary's *perpetual* virginity), it seems strange when we take the whole Bible into account.

You'll have to give me help in bringing the whole Bible to bear on this question.

There's no mention of other children when the holy family made the trip to Jerusalem and the twelve-year-old Jesus got lost. It's highly unlikely that a Jewish mother would leave her younger children at home while traveling to another city with her eldest. In Mark 3:20-21 and John 7:2-5, the relatives of Jesus are shown telling him what to do. The customs of the time wouldn't allow younger brothers in the same family to talk like that to their big brother. And if Mary had other sons besides Jesus, why would he, when he was dying (John 19:27), have handed her over to the care of John, who wasn't a member of the immediate family?

But how would you explain the confusion then?

Let's start with a close look at the names of those present on Calvary. Mark 15:40 lists among the three women standing there a "Mary the mother of James the younger and Joses." No one thinks that this Mary, despite the same name, was Mary the mother of Jesus. If she had been, Mark would surely have come right out and identified her as such, as the mother of the crucified Jesus rather than as the mother of two others who played no part in this scene. Now recall that in Mark 6:3 these same two names had appeared among the "brothers." But that means that these sons of the *other* Mary weren't sons of Mary, Jesus' mother, and so weren't really his blood brothers.

That's helpful. Anything else?

Another opinion is that the "brothers of the Lord" were sons of Joseph by a former marriage. But there's no evidence of this in the Gospels. In fact, one reason why Matthew features Joseph so strongly in the infancy narrative is because it's through him that Jesus has legal claim to royal lineage as son of David. But if Joseph had older sons, wouldn't they take precedence in the royal line and compromise Jesus' Davidic claims? At the very least, it's highly unlikely something so important would be casually overlooked in Matthew's Gospel, written for a Jewish-Christian audience.

What about the words in the original? Could they have been mistranslated?

While the Greek word *adelphos* normally means a blood brother (and *adelphe* means a blood sister), that's not always true. In Romans 9:3, it means "co-religionist," in Matthew 5:22-24, "neighbor," in Mark 6:17-18, "step-brother," in Genesis 29:12, 24:48, "kinsman, relative."

Modern biblical scholarship, then, would at times allow a broad interpretation for *adelphos* and *adelphe*. They can sometimes be translated as "relative," "kinsman," or other similar words. And when account is taken of the very ancient (second century A.D.) and very strong tradition (practically unanimous for centuries) of "Mary *ever virgin*," the question is answered. Did Jesus have any brothers and sisters? According to the flesh, no. According to the Spirit, we sincerely hope he has a multitude, ourselves included: " . . . Whoever does the will of my heavenly Father is brother and sister and mother to me" (Matthew 12:50).

19. The Protestant Lord's Prayer

I have noticed that Catholics and Protestants have different ways of praying the Our Father. Protestants add on "For thine is the kingdom and the power and the glory forever." Which version is truly the Lord's own prayer, the one he wanted us to pray?

If you look up Matthew 6:9-13 and Luke 11:2-4 in your Bible, you will find two different versions of the Lord's Prayer. Luke's version is shorter than Matthew's, but Matthew's is the one we popularly use.

It is wholly natural for any person to use somewhat different wordings each time he or she explains the same matter on many different occasions. Jesus most likely talked to his followers about prayer many, many different times. His explanations would hardly have been formulated in identical words and phrases each time. But, despite many differences in exact wording, Jesus' basic ideas about prayer would have remained the same.

This basic teaching of Jesus (about prayer, as well as about all other topics) was remembered and treasured and handed down from one generation of disciples to the next. Just as Jesus' own teaching was surely not limited to one fixed set of words only, so also the tradition, the handing on of his teaching, was more probably formulated in a variety of ways. Finally, as a result, differing formulations or versions came to be set down in written form when our Gospels were composed about thirty-five to sixty years after the earthly lifetime of Jesus.

Are there some scriptural versions that are closer to the actual words of Christ? And how do we know which they are?

Even if there are sections of the Gospels that actually contain the exact words that Jesus himself used, we have no way of finding out with certainty which sections those might be. But it really makes no difference. We do know that in the Gospels we have Jesus' basic ideas, his basic attitudes, his basic teachings. That's what really counts, not his exact wording.

Actually, in the case you asked about — "For thine is the kingdom and the power and the glory forever" — it was added to the Our Father by Catholics some generations after the New Testament had been written. Later, this addition fell out of general use only to be rediscovered again by the Protestant churches at the time of the Reformation. And when we look at the liturgy of the

Mass since Vatican II, it looks like we have come full circle; for now, shortly after the Lord's Prayer, we add: "For the kingdom, the power and the glory are yours, now and for ever."

Wait a minute. I would like to go back to something you said — that Catholics added the phrase "after the New Testament was written." Aren't you introducing a new idea here?

That's true. So, maybe it will be clearer if I sum it up for you. What we have here are different wordings of the Lord's Prayer before the Gospels were ever written (most likely different wordings by Jesus himself from one occasion to the next), different wordings within the Gospels themselves, and different wordings after the Gospels were composed, right up to our own times. (No one claims that the phrase about the kingdom and the power is word for word in the New Testament, but it certainly has a biblical flavor.) But, and this is what's most important, all of these versions are faithful to our Lord's basic teachings, faithful to what Jesus tried to get across to his followers. Through and in Christ, risen and living today, the Church is assured of this by the guidance of the Holy Spirit. The activity of the Holy Spirit does not imply that we are necessarily in possession of Jesus' own exact words and phrases. The presence of the Holy Spirit, however, does guarantee that the Church receives divine guidance to understand Christ's teaching more fully and more deeply. John's Gospel expresses this confidence in these words:

> I have much more to tell you,
> but you cannot bear it now.
> When he comes, however,
> being the Spirit of truth
> he will guide you to all truth . . . " (John 16:12-13).

By this special help from God, the Church keeps faithful to the basic ideas and teachings of Jesus.

20. The End Time

What does the Catholic Church have to say about the Book of Revelation? I heard a preacher claim that many of the prophecies in that book are happening right now. He said that we are jeopardizing our salvation by not recognizing this. I don't remember ever hearing anything about this from a Catholic source.

If a prize were given for the most misinterpreted book of the Bible, the winner, hands down, would be the Book of Revelation. No other part of God's Word has been so abused or had its original message so misunderstood as this last book of the Bible.

What is there about this book, inspired though it is, that makes its lessons so easy to misapply?

One reason would be its unusual literary style. It's called "prophetic apocalyptic," and we have nothing like it in our literature. It flourished in the Middle East for 400 years, from 200 B.C. to A.D. 200. When John, the human author of this book, wanted to deliver a powerful message to the churches of Asia Minor, he adapted this already familiar style for his own purposes. Since the people of those days knew how this dramatic style worked, he didn't worry that they would misunderstand the coded messages he was using.

But we are living 1,900 years later and in an entirely different culture. If we try to grasp this book with our usual thought processes, it won't work.

Well, at least we still understand what prophecy means. Don't we?

I'm not so sure we do. A prophet in Scripture is not principally a predictor of the future; rather, he is a spokesman for God. Modern scholarship tells us that the Book of Revelation was interpreting events that were happening at that time, namely, the first-century persecution of the Christians by the Roman authorities. John was dealing with current events of the early Church: " . . . for the appointed time is near!" (Revelation 1:3)

But there's so much of Revelation that seems purposefully hidden and mysterious. What's the key to it?

The key lies in the use of symbols that were much better understood at the time: numbers, personalities and events, crisis situations, the elements of the earth. Some of the key numeric symbols are: seven = perfection; six = imperfection; twelve = the New Israel; four = the world; a thousand = a round number implying immensity. Also, numerical values were assigned to the letters of the Hebrew alphabet, and when these numbers were added together they stood for a name. This brings us to the Bible's most misunderstood number: 666. Obviously, almost any name, with a little manipulation, could be made to total this infamous number of the beast. Some candidates of the past have been the pope, Muhammed, Luther, Napoleon, Hitler, and Stalin. (Emperor Nero was most probably the one intended.) It's a natural form of human prejudice to want evidence in God's Word for one's own side, but that doesn't make it any less an abuse of Scripture.

Does this book have anything to say to modern Christians?

Yes, a prayerful approach, perhaps with the aid of a good commentary, will help us realize that there is a message of hope here for oppressed people of all times. This sacred text can remind us that, as Christians, we are called upon today to do battle with all the dehumanizing and exploitative forces present in our society.

That's why, after we read the Book of Revelation, we should return to the Gospels. There we'll see the Son of Man returning, not just at the end of time but now, in the work of those who feed the hungry, give drink to the thirsty, clothe the naked, and harbor the homeless. It's caring Christians such as these who can joyfully cry out Revelation's closing prayer: " . . . Come, Lord Jesus!" (Revelation 22:20)

21. Paraclete: What Does It Mean?

> I have real trouble with some of the words in the Bible. They don't even seem to be translated — like the word "Paraclete." What does it mean when the Bible has Jesus say:
> If you love me
> and obey the commands I give you,
> I will ask the Father
> and he will give you another Paraclete —
> to be with you always" (John 14:15-16)?

You're right. That's a very foreign word — a Greek word — that we've simply carried over into our English translations. We've done so because of one of the basic problems of translating in general. When a word is translated into another language, only rarely is the *exact* meaning achieved. Usually, there are nuances, overtones, or associations that don't come across in the new language. When, because of this, the original "foreign" term has been kept, as in this case, it retains all of its meaning, but that meaning remains "packed away" in it and has to be unpacked. It's a good thing to learn to do.

> So, how do I go about getting the sense of a strictly biblical term?

Let's stay concrete. In this case, you would have to collect the various bits that make up the total sense of the word from the other words that Scripture uses to describe the role of the one here called "the Paraclete," that is, the Holy Spirit.

If I promise to search the New Testament later, would you give me some idea of what I'll find?

Sure. The Holy Spirit's role is described as that of advocate, healer, intercessor, defender, "one who speaks up for another," mediator, teacher, consoler, friend. I know that doesn't add up to an exact definition; but, perhaps more important, it gives us a "feel" for the word.

Then, too, since the Holy Spirit is called "another" Paraclete in the text you quoted, Jesus must be the first Paraclete. That means we can set up a parallelism along these lines: what Jesus was for his disciples — defender, helper, teacher, mediator, friend, etc. — is what the Holy Spirit will be for the Christian community. Think of what that means. John's Gospel is describing a special role for the Spirit, namely, as the personal presence of Jesus in the Christian community while Jesus is with the Father. Our Savior has ascended into heaven; but he hasn't left us orphans — he has sent us his Spirit. The Paraclete's principal work is to reveal the glorified Christ to the disciples and, through them, to the world. Because the Paraclete enables the disciples to carry on the work of Christ, they will experience the same rejection and persecution.

When we recall when this Gospel was written (probably between A.D. 90 and 95), these words about the Paraclete in their midst must have come across to a persecuted Church as very encouraging indeed. Also, they must have been very reassuring to a worried community who had just lost or was about to lose their leader, the "Beloved Disciple," their last link to the already distant Jesus of Nazareth. But the Gospel told them that it wasn't primarily the recollections of the eyewitnesses that counted. After all, the disciples had seen Jesus do many things, had heard him speak of God's kingdom, but had not really understood. Only the Spirit, given after the Resurrection, taught the meaning of what they had seen and heard. And to think, this very same Spirit was still with them as their Paraclete sixty years after the Lord's Ascension.

But what does all this really mean for today?

The key is the final word of the text you quoted, "always." The inspired words of the Gospel weren't meant only for the end of the first century. John's words about the Paraclete apply to the twentieth century also. The incredible message the evangelist was trying to convey was this: through the work of the Spirit, *it is possible for a Christian to know Christ far more fully and adequately now, after the Resurrection,* than he or she could have known Jesus by seeing him only in the days of his earthly life.

Some of this is quite new to me, and I have a problem with it, right off. This very active "role" for the Holy Spirit doesn't seem to fit with that other "picture" of him as dwelling in us as in a temple. That's biblical too, isn't it?

It certainly is biblical. Saint Paul said to the Christians of his day: "Are you not aware that you are the temple of God, and that the Spirit of God dwells in you?" (1 Corinthians 3:16) And I'm glad you brought it up. It gives us a chance to go back where we started.

Revelation is God's Word in human words. Since this is so and since no human word — biblical or otherwise — can completely describe what God is or does, we are left with words that give us only part of the picture. What this means is that, although he can be described as putting himself in our service in the role of Paraclete, our God remains, at the same time, the God of the first and greatest commandment that is to be served and adored in the temple of our hearts.

Actually, it is not only the Holy Spirit but also the Father and the Son who dwell in the souls of the just. Hence our Lord said:

> Anyone who loves me
> will be true to my word,
> and my Father will love him;
> we will come to him
> and make our dwelling place with him (John 14:23).

However, as a special act of God's love, this indwelling is attributed to the Holy Spirit.

If we grasp this truth deeply, it can alter our lives profoundly. How much easier, for instance, it will be to pray if we realize that we are speaking not to a distant God in heaven but to him who dwells right within our hearts, loving us and waiting for our love in return.

Again, in time of temptation or sorrow we turn for strength to God who dwells within us. Of ourselves we can do nothing. Without his grace, our minds can neither enter the world of faith nor surrender, in confidence, our lives to Jesus. But he will give us the strength we need to overcome temptation and to bear the trials and sorrows of life. " . . . He (God) will not let you be tested beyond your strength. Along with the test he will give you a way out of it so that you may be able to endure it" (1 Corinthians 10:13).

It is precisely in order to join us to him in the bonds of love that God abides within our hearts. In this way we begin here on earth the life that we will live throughout eternity in heaven.

Dear reader: If you have found this book helpful, it is due to the fact that it deals with concerns that have surfaced in actual discussions and correspondence with real people — just like you — who did not hesitate to share their difficulties about the Bible. If you have similar questions, I'd appreciate hearing from you. You can help me serve others. *Write:* Father Patrick Kaler, Liguori Publications, One Liguori Drive, Liguori, Missouri 63057.